CONTENTS

GENERAL LEARNING OBJECTIVES OF THIS UNIT

This Open Learning Unit will supply you with all the core information you need for an introduction to the area. It is likely that it will take you about 4 hours to work through, though if you undertake all the suggested activities it might well take longer.

By the end of this Unit, you should:

 have gained a general overview of the major areas of cognitive psychology;

▷ be able to identify some of the main theoretical concepts within the different areas of cognition;

▷ have some understanding of how psychological knowledge of cognitive processes can be applied to practical problems.

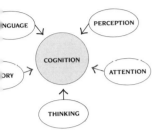

What are cognitive processes?

'You're coming home on the bus. You're tired, so you're just sitting there, letting your thoughts drift. The bus stops and some people get on. Idly, you watch as a couple of elderly white ladies fumble with their purses and eventually find the money for their fares. The queue moves on, as the new passengers go through the routine of paying their fares and moving to seats. But then the rhythm is interrupted. The driver's voice sounds louder, and harsh. You start paying attention. An Asian lady appears to be having difficulty with her fare, and the driver, who is white, is clearly impatient. She becomes more and more flustered, but eventually finds the fare, and goes to take her seat.

As the next passenger pays the fare, you think about what just happened. Why was the driver so intolerant? Was he being racist? You remember that he hadn't been stroppy with the elderly white ladies, and they had taken just as long to pay. In a discussion later, you describe the incident to your friends. You agree that you can't be certain, but that it probably was racism.'

Obviously, there's a lot going on in this episode. It raises questions on all sorts of levels: social (in terms of what is going on between those people), individual (in terms of what particular individuals are like), and societal (in terms of how our wider society works). All human interaction works on lots of levels, and if we were to try to understand everything that was going on, we'd have to look at each of them — which would fill up a very much larger book than this! In this Unit, though, we are interested in how we use cognition* to understand what is going on around us. Cognition is to do with thinking and understanding — it's the study of how the mind works. We are continually receiving information from our surroundings, but what do we do with that information once we've received it? How come we notice some things, but not others? What exactly are we doing when we think about the things that we've seen? What goes on in the mind?

Let's take a look at the cognitive processes which you, as the observer, might have used during the incident which I described earlier.

Perception

At first, you are simply watching what is happening. This involves the cognitive process of perception*, as you take in what is around you, identify shapes and forms as being human beings and features of the environment, and match up what you are observing to what you would generally expect to observe in a similar situation.

Attention

When the event stops matching up with your expectations, you become more alert. You begin actively to take in what is happening — to notice it, rather than simply to observe it in passing. This cognitive process is known as attention*.

Thinking

Later, you think about it. The cognitive process of thinking* involves working out what has just happened, bringing into play your previous knowledge and your general understanding of the situation. In other words, you treat the event as a social problem which needs to be solved.

Memory

You don't just think about it, but you also remember it. The cognitive process of memory* comes into play, as you store your knowledge of what happened, and the interpretations that you put on it. Later, you retrieve the information from your memory, when you are with your friends.

Language

Finally, telling your friends about it involves using language*. You find words which will express your thinking, and choose those which you feel will best convey to your friends the situation as you see it. In order to do this, you are using words to define what happened, as well as simply to describe it, and so the language that you use and the way that you think about the incident become very closely connected.

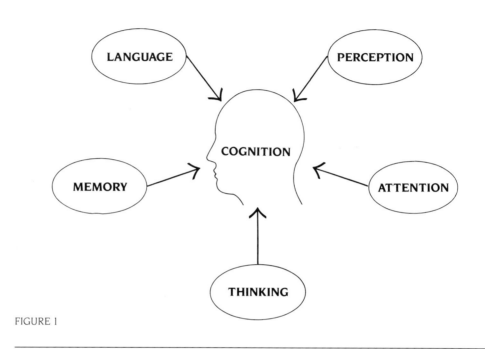

FIGURE 1

 SOMETHING TO TRY

Together with a friend, think of an event which has happened to you both recently, and try to work out all the different ways that cognitive processes might have been involved in your experiences. Do it separately, and then compare your two lists. Did you both think of the same processes?

In this set of six Open Learning Units, we will be exploring each of these different aspects of cognition. As we've just seen, each of them plays a part in everyday life: we engage in perception, attention, thinking, memory and language all the time. As human beings, we tend to react to what we believe is happening — and sometimes this isn't the same as what is really taking place! As you study cognition in more detail, you'll see that sometimes this can mean that two people respond very differently to the same event or stimulus. Most of the time, though, we are pretty accurate in working out what is going on around us. This may become clearer as we take a look at each of the main areas of cognition in more detail.

SAQ
1

1. *What are the five major areas of cognition?*

2. *Outline, in order, the cognitive processes which you would use if you were telling your friends about something that you saw earlier on in the day?*

3. *What is cognition?*

Perception

By perception we mean how information that has been received through the senses is interpreted and understood.

The processes of perception

The processes of perception involve the brain decoding and making sense of the information that it is receiving, in such a way that the information can be acted upon, or stored. That means that, if we want to understand perception, we need to look at three things:

- how we receive the information in the first place;
- how we group together different bits of information to work out what they are representing;
- how we combine all that with our previous knowledge, so that it will make sense to us.

How many senses are there?

We receive information through our senses — and here I may have a surprise for you. Contrary to popular belief, human beings don't have five senses; they have at least six. We have the five senses which we use to receive information from the outside world: sight, hearing, touch, taste, and smell. But we also have senses that receive information from within our own bodies: the kinaesthetic senses*, which tell us about movement, or the feel of our muscles and joints. Some psychologists believe that these internal senses can be classified into three or four different kinds, but for now we will simply group them together.

Table 1. **THE SENSES**

Sense	Sense organs / receptors	Ability
Visual	the eye	to see
Auditory	the ear	to hear
Tactile	receptors in the skin	to feel external objects by touch
Olfactory	receptors in the nose	to smell
Gustatory	taste buds on the tongue	to taste
Kinaesthetic	receptors in the muscles and joints	to feel muscular tension; angles and movements of limbs and torso

Sensory modes*

It's important to include the internal senses as well as the external ones when we are studying cognition, because we are continually linking together information that has been gained through different modes. A mode is the term we use when we want to describe one particular way that perceptual information can be perceived. So, for instance, something you see is information which is received through the visual mode, whereas something you hear is information which is received through the auditory mode. There is always a great deal of cross-modal transfer*, as information which has been obtained from one mode, like sight, is applied to information gained through a different mode, like hearing or touch.

3

SOMETHING TO TRY

Try experimenting with safe food colourings, to see if cross-modal transfer will affect the sense of taste. What happens if you colour a lemon drink red? Will people recognise the taste? And what happens if you already know what it is — does it still taste the same?

Visual perception

When we are studying perception, though, we tend to concentrate on just one sense at a time. Most research has been done on visual perception, because that is the most important sense for human beings, so in these Open Learning Units we will mostly concentrate just on visual perception. In particular, we ask ourselves: how is it that we know what we are looking at?

1. *List the six major sensory systems of the body.*
2. *What is cross-modal transfer?*
3. *What sensory mode has been most studied by psychologists?*

Figure – ground discrimination

First, we will be looking at some of the basic mechanisms of perception. Visual information comes to us in the form of light waves, reaching the eye as a pattern of different wavelengths and varying brightness. Somehow, we have to sort all this out, and the first way that we seem to do this is by sorting it out into figures against backgrounds. So, instead of seeing just a mass of patches of different colours, we can distinguish objects and shapes. This is known as figure-ground discrimination*. It is possible that some aspects of this are built into the visual system. Hubel and Wiesel (1968, 1979) showed that there are special cells in the brain which help us to sort out visual information by identifying simple shapes and lines.

Silhouettes or vase?

The computational theory of perception

But simple shapes and lines aren't enough to explain how we recognize more complex objects. We also have to use the visual information that we have to calculate boundaries and edges, so that we can organize visual information into forms and shapes. The computational theory of perception* shows us one way that we might do this, by computing the data into simple 'stick-figure' representations of objects or people, and then building them up into more complete images by including more sophisticated detail.

Perceptual constancies

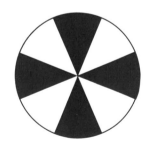

FIGURE 2. *Is it a black cross on a white background, or a white cross on a black background? It's both, but not at the same time. When you're looking at the black figure, the white one disappears, and vice versa. You see a **figure** against a **background**.*

The computational theory is concerned with showing how we can make sense out of the factual visual information that we receive. But sometimes, the psychological experience of perception isn't the same as the physical stimulus. For example, if you see someone a long way down the street, and then they walk towards you, the image on the retina grows steadily larger. But you don't perceive the person as growing larger, do you? Instead, you apply your knowledge of how visual information works, and simply put the change down to distance. This is one of the mechanisms of perceptual constancy* which help us to make sense out of what we see. There are other mechanisms, too, like the *principle of closure*, which describes our tendency to 'close up' incomplete figures, so that we see them as complete units and not just isolated bits.

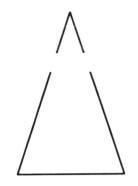

FIGURE 3. *Principle of closure.*

SAQ 3

Table 2. **PERCEPTUAL CONSTANCIES**

Size constancy	Knowledge of the 'real' size of the object means that distant objects seem larger than would be implied by the size of the retinal image being received.
Shape constancy	Knowledge of the 'real' shape of the object means that it is still perceived as being the same regardless of the angle from which it is viewed.
Colour constancy	Knowledge of the 'real' colour of the object means that it is still perceived as being the same colour, regardless of the actual colour wavelength of the light that reaches the eye.
Location constancy	Knowledge that objects don't generally move means that things are seen as remaining in the same place even when the observer moves around and the retinal image changes.

1. What is figure–ground discrimination?

2. According to the computational theory, what type of visual representations form the basis of shape perception?

3. What are perceptual constancies?

Visual illusions

Some psychologists have argued that we can learn a great deal about how perception works by looking at what happens when it goes wrong. Studying visual illusions may tell us about the general principles which we apply to visual

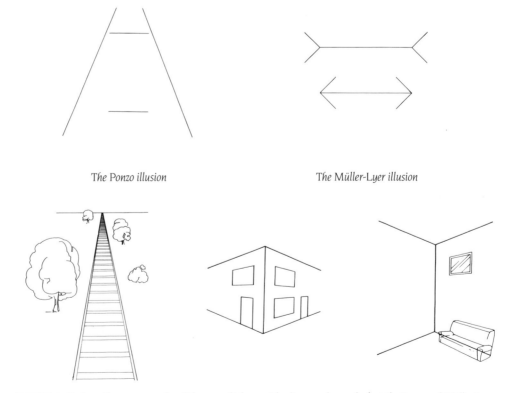

The Ponzo illusion   The Müller-Lyer illusion

FIGURE 4. *Perhaps these are examples of the cues which are misleading us when we look at the Ponzo and Müller-Lyer illusions.*

information, because illusions can show us how we can be misled. The hypothesis-testing theory of perception* shows how we can draw from our general knowledge of these principles to see things as we do. So, for instance, it explains geometric illusions as causing us to apply our perceptual constancies in the wrong way.

SOMETHING TO TRY

Collect as many different examples of visual illusions as you can, and see if you can group them into sets. Can you suggest explanations as to how any of them might work?

Direct perception

Gibson's theory of direct perception*, though, argues that perception in the real world isn't as much of a problem as all that. Because we are active in the real world, we can move around in it, and we can see things from several different angles. This gives us a great range of cues, such as changes in the apparent texture of objects, or the apparent motion of distant and near objects relative to one another. These cues allow us to perceive objects and our environment with very little uncertainty.

Face recognition

There has been quite a lot of recent research into face recognition — how we recognize other people, or how we interpret the faces of strangers. It's an interesting and important area of perceptual research for many reasons. For one thing, it shows how closely our perception matches our social needs. All human beings need to recognize the people that they deal with in everyday life, and almost effortlessly, we can tell people apart on the basis of minute differences in their faces — even though, objectively, those differences are sometimes tiny! Also, understanding face recognition means being able to integrate direct information about the visual stimulus (known as 'bottom-up' information), with other types of knowledge, like our ideas of people's identities, theories about character and personality, and interpretations of facial expression (known as 'top-down' information).

SAQ
4

1. *How can visual illusions be useful in studying perception?*
2. *What does the theory of direct perception say about the importance of movement?*
3. *What two types of theory can be integrated in the study of face recognition?*

3 Attention

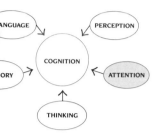

'Pay attention!'

'Look at me when I'm speaking to you!'

'Excuse me, but I couldn't help overhearing ...'

Ever heard these phrases before? I suspect you will have done, probably more than once. Each of them is to do with attention. And each of them tells us something different. Let's look at each in turn.

'Pay attention!'

This phrase tells us that it is possible to decide to pay attention to something — we can do it deliberately. We can also choose not to pay attention if we don't feel like doing so. Whether you decide to attend to what someone else is saying is up to you; and the teacher or supervisor who instructs you to 'Pay attention!' is aware of this. They are instructing you to keep your mind on the subject, and not to think about anything else.

FIGURE 5. 'Pay attention!' © Brenda Brin Booker

Sustained attention

But how long can you keep that up? A considerable amount of research has gone into studying sustained attention*, and how long people can maintain their concentration before they start making mistakes. This research has contributed a great deal to practical questions, such as how to design aircraft cockpits to make sure that pilots make as few mistakes as possible when looking at their instruments for hours on end.

Maintaining vigilance

Research into sustained attention has often involved asking people to undertake lengthy vigilance* tasks, like looking out for a special image to appear on a screen, and to give a signal when it occurs. You can tell whether the person is paying attention or not by counting the number of signals which they have missed. Early researchers found that there were a number of influences on how long people could concentrate. These could be grouped into signal factors* — factors which were concerned with the physical design and layout of the control panel; and motivational factors*, which were concerned with the person doing the task, such as whether they were being watched by someone else, and so on.

Table 3. FACTORS AFFECTING SUSTAINED ATTENTION

Signal factors	Motivational factors
Intensity of the signal	Feedback about how well the subject had performed (either true or false)
Duration of the signal	Occasional interruptions (e.g. phone ringing)
Presentation	
Frequency of signal	Presence of other people in the room
Spatial probability (e.g. whether it was in the centre of the display or near the edges)	Presence of high-status observer

The arousal theory of sustained attention

One theory which was put forward to explain some of the findings was the arousal* theory of sustained attention. This suggested that how long people can concentrate has a lot to do with how worked up they are — if they are too relaxed, they might not pay attention fully, but if they are overwrought, they might also make mistakes. The best state to be in was somewhere in between the two — not too relaxed but not too worked up either. Researchers found that getting the balance is important if people are to avoid making serious mistakes.

1. *Describe one practical application of research into sustained attention.*

2. *What do we mean by the term vigilance?*

3. *What can the arousal theory tell us about sustained attention?*

'*Look at me when I'm speaking to you!*'

The second phrase tells us that people expect certain actions, particularly eye-contact, when someone is paying attention. There are other behavioural* and physiological correlates of attention as well*. If we are paying attention to somebody, we tend to stay very still to minimize distraction, and to turn towards them in order to hear and see them better. There are changes in the patterns of muscle activity, in blood pressure and in heart rate. Although these changes can be very small, they seem to prepare us for action if it is needed, which gives us a clue as to why or how attentional mechanisms might have evolved.

Brain activity. Researchers have also found that there are changes in brain activity which happen when we are paying attention. Studies of electro-encephalograms* have shown that when we are paying attention to something the pattern of brain waves is different. Many studies have examined evoked potentials*, which are changes in electrical brain activity brought about by a single stimulus (like a dot of light); and these too have been helpful in building up our understanding of what is happening when we are paying attention to something.

FIGURE 6. 'Look at me when I'm speaking to you!' © Kester J. Eddy, Barnabys Picture Library.

Dividing attention

Psychologists have also investigated how we go about dividing our attention, so that we can do more than one thing at a time. This has involved research into how we acquire skills, and how we develop automatic routines for familiar tasks, so that they don't seem to need much attention at all. Capacity theory* is concerned with how much we can pay attention to at any given time, and how this may change depending on how motivated or aroused we are.

SAQ
6

1. *Describe two behavioural correlates of attention.*

2. *What are evoked potential recordings used for?*

3. *What is capacity theory?*

'*Excuse me, but I couldn't help overhearing ...*'

The third phrase describes a very different phenomenon. If we 'couldn't help overhearing', it implies that normally we wouldn't be listening, but that there was something unusual this time. And that implies that we can channel our attention, so that we notice some things and not others. *Selective attention* is rather special because, throughout our lives, we are continually selecting and interpreting the information that we receive. If we tried to pay attention to everything equally, we'd simply become overwhelmed.

9

FIGURE 7. 'Excuse me. I couldn't help overhearing!' © Brenda Brin Booker

---

SOMETHING TO TRY

Try writing down all the different things which your senses are telling you about at any one moment. This would include things that you generally ignore, for instance the feel of your clothes, or the colour of the walls. Use the list of sensory modes in Table 1 as a guide. Then underline the ones which you are normally aware of when you are relaxed (not when you're concentrating on something). How much do you normally filter out?

Filter theories of attention

Somehow, we need to find a way of sorting out that information, and there have been several theories which have suggested ways that we do this. Filter theories* propose that we operate a kind of 'bottleneck', so that not all of the information that we receive can come in to be processed, and some of it is filtered out. One early filter theory of selective attention proposed that we channel information according to its physical characteristics*. So, for instance, we might pay attention to things that we hear just through one ear, and ignore what we hear through the other one.

The cocktail party phenomenon

But sometimes, as the phrase showed, other information intrudes upon our notice. This is known as the cocktail party phenomenon*, and it's particularly likely to happen if you hear your own name, or if the person that you overhear is talking about something that you are very interested in. The question is, how does your attention become attracted even though this information has different physical characteristics from the thing you are attending to? How does your brain choose what you will pay notice to and what you will ignore?

The attenuation model

In an attempt to explain how this happens, Triesman proposed an attenuation model*, which suggested that we don't exactly filter information out, but that we filter it in such a way that it becomes weaker. This means that most information won't be noticed, but if it is particularly important, like our own name, then it will be picked up.

Late-selection models of attention

The attenuation model implies that all the information that we receive is scanned in some way for meaning, even if it is in the form of a very weak signal. But late-selection models of attention* suggest that, if we process everything for meaning, then there isn't any need for a filter at all. Instead, we can simply process all the information that we receive for meaning, and then decide what we pay attention to afterwards. We retain what is relevant, and we discard what isn't.

The perceptual cycle

Ulrich Neisser, on the other hand, argued that paying attention isn't a matter of filtering information out at all. Instead, we search actively for information, based on our previous experiences and what we have come to expect. The perceptual cycle* shows how we don't just receive information passively. We develop anticipatory schemata*, which provide us with a kind of 'plan' of what is likely to happen. This guides us in choosing what we will receive from our environment. In turn, the information that we receive adjusts and modifies our schemata, and channels what we will look for next. It is information which contradicts or challenges an anticipatory schema which particularly attracts our notice, and causes us to redirect our attention.

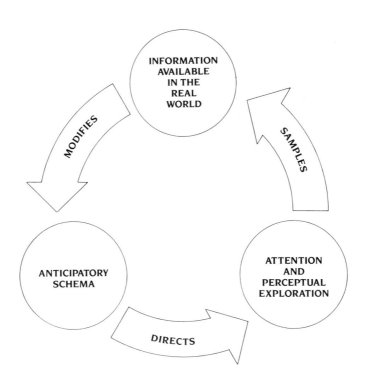

FIGURE 8. *Neisser's model of the perceptual cycle. Adapted from* **Cognition and Reality** (1976), U. Neisser. *San Francisco: W.H. Freeman.*

SAQ
7

1. *How did the first filter theories assert that information was selected?*
2. *What is the cocktail party phenomenon?*
3. *Describe the perceptual cycle.*

Thinking

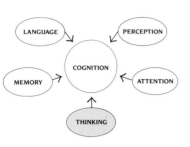

FIGURE 9. *Thinking.*

Have you ever seen a picture of Rodin's 'The Thinker'? It's a sculpture of a man sitting, head bowed, resting his knuckles on his forehead. In fact, even if you didn't know, I doubt if you'd need to be told what it was called. He looks so much the picture of intense concentration that you'd recognize instantly that that was what he was doing — thinking.

But thinking doesn't mean just sitting still and working something out mentally. That's one form of it, yes, but there are many more. In fact, we use the term 'thinking' to describe so many different mental activities that it's almost impossible to define it comprehensively. So psychologists who have studied thinking have tended to look at just one particular aspect of it, to find out what that involves.

Problem solving

One way of looking at how human beings think is to look at how they go about solving problems. Early research in this area showed that people often develop mental sets*, which mean that they become prepared to think about problems in a particular way. This can be helpful, because it means that you can apply your previous experience to a puzzle and solve it much more quickly. Sometimes, though, and particularly with a new type of problem, it is a hindrance, because it prevents you from thinking about the problem in a different way.

Mental sets

There are all sorts of different ways that people can develop such mental sets. For example, you might become fixed in your ideas about the function of an object, so that you can't see that it could be used for something entirely different; or you might end up applying one particular formula for getting solutions which you know will be successful, and not noticing that there is a short-cut which is much quicker. Studies of mental sets have told us a great deal about thinking styles: some people seem to be good at lateral thinking*, for instance, which involves being able to look at a problem from a completely different angle from the one which we would normally use.

SOMETHING TO TRY

Try asking several different people how many uses they can think of for a soup-bowl. (Ask yourself, first.) Some people's lists are likely to be much longer than others: why is that? What might it tell us about the different ways that people think?

Human reasoning

Another aspect of the study of thinking involves looking at reasoning and logic*. With human beings, these aren't necessarily the same thing. People don't always reason logically: we have systematic cognitive biases* in our thinking, which mean that we tend to be quite bad at processing negative information. So, for example, it takes longer to understand the sentence 'the students were given neither books nor paper' than it does to understand 'the students were given books and paper'.

1. *Give one advantage and one disadvantage of mental sets.*

2. *What is lateral thinking?*

3. *Describe one human bias in processing information.*

Applying social knowledge

We also tend to apply our wider *social knowledge* to logical problems which involve people. So where a computer, acting with a strict logic, might draw one conclusion, a human being might draw a different one, because we would add in our knowledge of people and how they generally act. This isn't necessarily a bad thing. It can certainly be helpful to us in predicting how other people will act. If we look at thinking as something which has evolved gradually in our species, through natural selection, we might even argue that predicting how people will act is what it is for. An animal which can predict how others will behave stands a much better chance of surviving than one which can't, after all.

FIGURE 10. *'Now, let me see. First he usually hides behind the tree, then he moves across to the rock, and then ...'*
© Brenda Brin Booker

Computer simulation

Computers work by applying formal rules to problems, and there's been quite a lot of work on computer simulation* of problem-solving tasks. Some of this work has been very helpful in letting us know about the types of logical jumps which people can make. These often involve applying heuristics* — short-cuts to solving a problem which are chosen because they look as though they might

13

pay off. Human beings can also take several different factors into account at once when they are thinking about a problem, and recent work on parallel distributed processing* (PDP) in computer systems has tried to mimic that too.

Artificial intelligence

Many psychologists have been involved with research into artificial intelligence*. This involves attempting to develop computer systems which can replicate or substitute for human intelligence in particular tasks. Some of this research is concerned with developing expert systems* designed to provide relevant information which will help experts to make better decisions, like producing a list of illnesses involving a particular symptom to help a doctor to make a diagnosis.

1. *Describe one limitation to computer problem solving in comparison with that of human beings.*
2. *What are heuristics?*
3. *Describe one area of research into artificial intelligence.*

Representation

A different branch of the study of thinking is concerned with representation*. Representation refers to how we code information mentally. For instance, it's unlikely that you think of your next-door neighbour by using the actual words 'next-door neighbour'. You're more likely to have some kind of mental picture, or image, which you conjure up when you think of them. We seem to develop different types of representation as we grow older, perhaps because the kind of information that we have to deal with becomes much more complex. An important part of thinking involves manipulating these mental representations, combining and recombining them to help us to get new insights.

Table 4. **FORMS OF REPRESENTATION**

Form	Nature	Observation
Enactive	Information is stored as actions or 'muscle memories'.	Probably the main type of mental representation for young infants.
Iconic	Information is stored as sensory images, often pictures.	Develops in childhood, and is often very strong. Its most extreme form is eidetic (photographic) imagery.
Symbolic	Information is stored using symbols to 'stand for' the idea.	Develops more fully in adolescence, and allows for the development of conceptual, abstract, and imaginative thought.

Concept formation

One way of representing a mass of information is to group it into concepts. We do this on the basis of its being similar in some way. Then we use these concepts in our thinking, applying them to our understanding of other information. Some concept formation* theories propose that we classify things together on the basis of the features that they have in common, matching them up to some common pattern, or template. Other psychologists have suggested that we tend to form concepts on the basis of what we do with an object, not what the object is like. So, for instance, we see something as a 'chair' not because it has four legs (there are chairs which have only three), but because we sit on it.

Schemas and scripts

This approach to concept formation can also be linked with some of the wider forms of representation which psychologists have studied. Schemas* and scripts* form action plans which guide us in understanding what is going on around us. For example, if we visit a restaurant, we have a kind of internal 'script' which tells us what should happen next, the sort of thing we can expect the waiter to say, and so on. Because we have this internal representation, and it is shared by the other people around us, we can manage to regulate social interaction quite easily.

Cognitive maps

Similarly, we develop internal representations about places and locations. Cognitive maps tell us where we are with respect to other places nearby, and help us to move around our environment effectively. They can also be important as 'triggers' for storing information, by providing useful cues for our memories. For example, one well-known technique for remembering lists is the 'method of loci', in which the items are remembered as being linked to particular points along a journey. The image that we have of their physical location helps us to recall the items.

 SOMETHING TO TRY

Just from memory, draw a map of your local town centre or shopping centre. You might get your friend to draw one, as well. Compare the two maps: are they similar? Then compare them with a printed map of the area. Did you get things the right size? Or were the places that you know well bigger than the ones that you don't?

---

1. *How might the use of concepts help us to think?*
2. *What is a 'script' in social life?*
3. *Describe the method of loci?*

5 Memory

How good is your memory? Can you remember where your best friend's house is? Do you remember what you had for breakfast this morning? Do you find it easy to remember things for exams?

Episodic and semantic memory

We use memory all the time, often quite unconsciously. If we didn't, we wouldn't even be able to look after ourselves, because we wouldn't be able to carry out planned sequences of actions, like making a cup of tea. But when we speak of having a 'good' or a 'bad' memory, we don't mean memory of that sort — making a cup of tea is not the kind of thing that people normally forget. Psychologists draw a distinction between episodic* and semantic memory*. Episodic memory is our memory for particular events — the how, when and where things happened; but semantic memory is much more concerned with skills, and how to do things. So, for example, if you were remembering what you did yesterday evening, that would be episodic memory. But if you were asked to operate a tape-recorder, or to write a letter, that would involve semantic memory, in the form of the skill-based knowledge of how to make the machinery work, or your even more skilled memory of how to use language.

Everyday memory

Most of the research which has been done on memory has been concerned with how we remember factual information, like the sort of material you might need to learn for an exam. Recently, though, psychologists have become more interested in everyday memory*, such as how we remember how to do things, or how memory lapses happen.

 SOMETHING TO TRY

Write down all of the different things you need to remember when you are making a cup of tea. Include everything you can think of, like what a teapot looks like, or how to lift something. Which of these are memory for facts, and which are skills? You might also get a friend to write a list too, so that you can compare them. Did you both think of the same things? How might you group the different kinds of memory together if you were trying to classify them?

Coding, storage and retrieval

When we are deliberately memorizing information, there are three stages involved. First we need to *code* the information, so that it can form some kind of mental representation. Once this is done, we *store* that information for a period of time, and then, on a later occasion, we *retrieve* it. Coding information may also involve making connections with other items of information, or changing its form in some way.

SAQ
11

1. *Distinguish between episodic and semantic memory.*

2. *Give two examples of everyday memory.*

3. *What are the three stages of memory?*

Forms of remembering

When we come to retrieve our memories, there are a number of different forms of remembering. These range from being able to draw something out of memory with hardly any prompting — known as free recall — to being unable to remember something consciously, but finding that it takes much less time to learn it a second time around. Recognizing information comes somewhere in between these two.

Table 5. **SOME FORMS OF REMEMBERING**

Recall.......................................Information is retrieved directly from memory at will.

Recognition.........................Information is identified as familiar when seen or heard again.

Reconstruction.................Information is re-organized into its original form, although
(Redintegration)   there is no conscious memory of having seen it before.

Re-learning savings.........Information which has been learned once takes less time to
                             be learned again than does new material, even though there
                             is no conscious recollection of it.

The two-process theory of memory

There have been a number of theories put forward to explain how memory storage takes place. The two-process theory of memory* suggests that we have two different types of memory. One of these is a very rapid, *short-term memory* (STM) which only holds a limited number of items and fades within a few seconds. The other is a *long-term memory* (LTM) store, which can hold a considerable amount of information, and for very much longer periods of time. This theory holds that the short-term store acts as an entry system for information to pass into long-term memory.

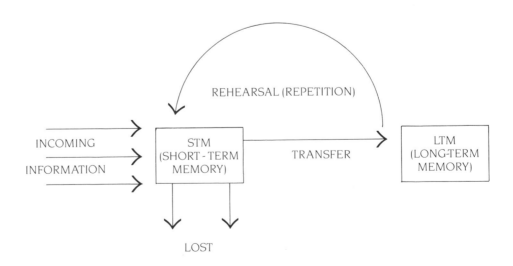

FIGURE 11. *The two-process theory of memory.*

Levels of processing

Craik and Lockhart (1973) believe that the reason why we only remember some things for very short periods of time, and others for longer, isn't because they are held in different stores, but because we process them less. If you're interested in an item of information — say it was something you heard about your best friend — you would process it. In other words, you would think about it, and what it meant, and what its implications were. You'd remember it. But if you weren't really interested much at all — say you heard the same thing about someone you didn't even know — then you wouldn't process it much at all, and you'd probably forget it very quickly. So the levels of processing theory* argues that it is what we do with the information which determines how well we will remember it.

SOMETHING TO TRY

Using the levels of processing model (the more you process information, the better you'll remember it), work out three different methods that you might use to help you to remember information when you're revising for exams. This might include changing the form of the information, or finding some way of making yourself think about the meaning and implications of what you are learning.

---

1. *Describe three different ways of remembering.*

2. *Draw a diagram illustrating the two-process theory of memory.*

3. *Briefly describe the levels of processing theory of memory.*

Working memory

Another way of looking at memory storage involves the concept of working memory*, which presents a model of memory in which the immediate memory is seen as being a bit like a computer's working memory. That's where changes take place, and where calculations or information processing are carried out, before the information is either put to use or put back into long-term storage.

Theories of forgetting

Another aspect of studying how we retrieve information is looking at what happens when retrieval breaks down. Why do we forget things? There are a number of *theories of forgetting*, ranging from forgetting which occurs because of brain damage or disease, to forgetting something because of interference from other information, to forgetting simply because we haven't had the right cues to remind us. Each of these explanations for why we forget can tell us something about how we retrieve our memories.

Table 6. **THEORIES OF FORGETTING**

Brain damage or decay...............Information is forgotten because the person's brain is physiologically damaged perhaps from head injury, or from neurological disorders, like Korsakoff's syndrome or Alzheimer's disease.

Motivated forgetting..................Information is forgotten because remembering it is personally disturbing or distressing to the individual.

Interference.................................Other information may become confused with, or interfere with, recall. This may occur proactively, with previously learned information making future learning difficult; or retroactively, with new learning interfering with the recall of past information.

Inadequate context and cues........Information may be difficult to retrieve because it was learned in an entirely different setting or context. Contexts may be internal or external. *State-dependent learning* is when memories set down in one state, for example, while drunk, only come back when the individual is in that state again, but are not available while they are sober.

Lack of processing......................Information may be forgotten because it was never used, or processed, in the first place. The more we 'work on' information that we come across, e.g. by thinking about its implications or changing its form, the less likely we are to forget it.

Memory as an active process

A different picture of how memory works comes through when we look at the way that people remember social or meaningful information. We find that, although we may remember a past event accurately, sometimes the memory has been changed in order to make it fit in better with our expectations. Memory isn't like a tape-recording: it is an *active process*. Although we might be accurate in remembering the gist of what has gone on, we are really very bad indeed at remembering details, which can sometimes make eyewitness testimony quite unreliable.

SAQ
13

1. *What is meant by the term working memory?*
2. *List five different theories of forgetting.*
3. *Explain what psychologists mean when they say that memory is an active process.*

6 Language

Imagine if you had no language. How would you get on? Think about all the things you do in a typical day. How many of them depend on being able to communicate with language? If you had no language at all, you would find it difficult to catch a bus, you wouldn't be able to read a book, to go shopping, to watch anything but simple pictures on television — in short, life would be severely limited.

Communicating abstract ideas

But we do have language. And in many ways, it's the most important of all of our human abilities, because it's through language that we can imagine other worlds. We're not just limited to the one we live in; we can do more than just describe what's around us. We can use language to communicate abstract ideas and alternative possibilities — and that's what has made human civilization possible.

FIGURE 12. 'So imagine, if we put a cathedral just there ...' © Brenda Brin Booker

How do language and thought relate?

But just what is the link between language and thinking? Does thinking depend on language? Or are they independent abilities, which come together when we engage in verbal thought? The early behaviourists* believed that thinking was nothing more than sub-vocal speech: that if you measured them very carefully, you would detect minute movements of the throat and larynx which were the speaking movements associated with each thought. Nowadays, this theory has been thoroughly discredited, but the question of how thinking and language are actually connected is still important.

SOMETHING TO TRY

Make tape-recordings of someone talking about their stereo system at some length. (Write out the words beforehand.) Get someone with a regional accent to read it out, and someone with a 'Standard English' accent. Play one of the recordings to some people, and the other to other people. When you have played it, ask each person to rate the speakers on a number of characteristics, including 'intelligence', 'pleasantness', 'practicality' and 'interest'. Is there any difference in people's judgements?

Accent and dialect

One reason why the question of the relationship between language and thought is important is because it has social implications. There have been a number of studies showing how accent* and dialect* affect how people are perceived. Even though our common sense may tell us that isn't true, it is surprising how often people who have very pronounced accents are judged as being less intelligent or less well educated than those who speak in more standard ways. There's an unconscious belief held by many people that our ability to think depends on how we use language.

1. *Describe two cognitive advantages which the ability to use language offers.*

2. *How did the early behaviourists account for language?*

3. *How may someone's accent affect how they are perceived?*

Linguistic relativity

It isn't just how we use language, either. One set of theories holds that we need to have the words for something before we can even begin to think about it. This is what is known as the strong form of the linguistic relativity hypothesis*, developed on the basis of anthropological work in non-technological societies. People in these societies seemed to think in very different ways from people in Western developed countries, and this was reflected in the languages which they used. So, for example, the Hopi Indian tribe used the same word to describe 'insect', 'air-pilot', and 'aeroplane', and some anthropologists concluded that this revealed how they thought of these different things in the same way, although this idea has been challenged recently.

Linguistic universals

Other anthropologists, though, argued that thinking wasn't completely determined by language. In particular, according to Berlin and Kay (1969) there seem to be some linguistic universals*, at least for direct forms of experience like colour names. Although different cultures may vary in terms of the number of words for colour that they have, the people who speak those languages can perform colour discrimination tasks just as well as those with wider vocabularies.

21

Verbal deprivation

Another form of the linguistic relativity hypothesis appeared in the theory of verbal deprivation*. This proposed that the type of language that we use determines how we think, so that if we speak in a restricted language code which has a different form (see Table 7) and doesn't use as many words, we only have access to certain forms of meaning. If we don't have the words to describe something, Bernstein believed, then we are not really able to think about it.

Table 7. **RESTRICTED AND ELABORATED CODES**

An Elaborated Code:	**A Restricted Code:**
is verbally explicit	is verbally implicit
doesn't depend on extra-linguistic features (e.g. tone of voice)	relies on extra-linguistic features
doesn't depend on the context	depends on the context in which it is used
is easily used for abstract concepts	is more appropriate for concrete, practical concepts
emphasizes individuality	emphasizes group membership
maintains social distance	strengthens social relationships
mainly middle-class speakers	mainly working-class speakers
is used in formal settings	is used in informal settings

Restricted and elaborated codes

Bernstein observed social class differences in the forms of language that people use, and argued that this meant that working-class people who used restricted codes* of language were disadvantaged in education, because their language limited their access to the more general and abstract concepts which are involved in higher forms of learning. Middle-class people, on the other hand, used elaborated language codes*, which allowed them to discuss more complicated and abstract ideas. This work was sharply criticized, through research which showed that the form of language that people used didn't make them any less able to think about abstract ideas.

---

1. *What does the phrase linguistic relativity hypothesis refer to?*

2. *What idea of the relationship between thinking and language is contained in the theory of verbal deprivation?*

3. *Compare elaborated and restricted codes of language.*

Language influences cognition

We can see, though, that even if it doesn't restrict what we can actually think, language does have the power to influence our cognitive processes to quite a high degree. Experimental studies have shown that language can influence memory, perception, and problem-solving. These studies imply that the form of language that we use can direct our thinking in certain directions, so that we don't notice alternative possibilities.

Sexist language

One area which shows this very clearly is sexist language. This shows how language can be used to maintain prejudice in society — and has parallels with the use of racist language too. The study of sexist language includes looking at how the range of vocabulary in a language influences how we perceive reality. For example, there are very few positive words in English to describe a woman with a strong character, although there are lots for describing men. This means that 'strong-minded' women are usually seen in some unpleasant way, using words like 'battleaxe' or 'cow'.

SOMETHING TO TRY

Find a passage in a textbook or encyclopaedia in which people are referred to as 'he', and human beings are referred to as 'man'. Re-write it, using the words 'she', and 'woman' throughout. Then read it out loud. Does it seem to have a different meaning? Does it seem as though the writer really meant everybody, including women, when talking about 'man'? Or does it seem as though it would only apply to males? How does this use of language colour our thinking?

Emotive language

Words often carry emotive overtones, which affect how we think of the subject that they are referring to. So, for example, if we hear the ruling body of a country spoken of as a 'regime' instead of a 'government', we may begin to think of that country in an entirely different way. And using words according to social conventions of this kind can lead to old-fashioned styles of social thinking being taken for granted. So, using 'he' to describe people of both sexes, for example, has often meant that women have been overlooked, both in everyday thinking, and in scientific theorizing.

DOREEN HAD BEEN **CLONING** HERSELF IN THE LABS AGAIN

FIGURE 13. *From 'Recycled images'.*

Language and thinking as overlapping independent processes

The great Russian developmental psychologist, Vygotsky, proposed that language and thinking start off as *independent processes*, but that as we become skilled at using language, it forms a tool which can help us in our thinking. Vygotsky argued that thinking begins when we need to restructure a situation mentally: we need to change the elements of the situation around in order to work out what is happening, or what might happen. Language, on the other hand, has social roots. Because we are social creatures, we need to be able to communicate with one another, and that is why we develop language. This can explain why sometimes, we know what we are thinking, but we find it hard to find words to express it, whereas at other times we seem to think in words. (It might also explain why sometimes we seem to speak without thinking at all!)

23

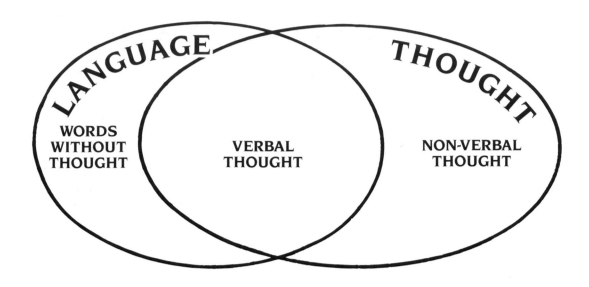

FIGURE 14. *Vygotsky's model of the relationship between language and thinking.*

1. *Give two examples of the use of sexist language.*
2. *How may emotive words influence our cognition?*
3. *What did Vygotsky consider to be the origins of thought?*

Factors influencing cognition

So what do we mean by cognition? As you can see, cognitive processes have been studied in many different ways, and from many different angles. Much of this research has been concerned with investigating how these processes work: the mental structures or mechanisms which we seem to use when we engage in perception, attention, thinking, memory, or language. But cognition doesn't just happen in a vacuum. It's closely linked with other aspects of our experience, too. If we try to disentangle the myriads of different influences which can affect our cognition, we can distinguish roughly three major strands: physiological factors, individual or personal factors, and social factors.

Physiological factors in cognition

Our cognition is sometimes directly affected by physiological processes. As we saw earlier, research into specialized cells in the visual cortex has shown that some of the component mechanisms involved in distinguishing figures against backgrounds may be directly 'wired in' to the nervous system. Similarly, research into attention has uncovered a number of physiological changes which occur when we are paying attention to something, and which act to enhance our receptivity to information and our readiness to act if necessary. Some psychologists have discovered that pictures of food appear brighter if we are hungry when we look at them; and neuropsychologists have shown how brain damage or disease can affect memory or speech.

Individual factors in cognition

Individual factors also influence cognitive processes: for instance, we remember information better if we have a personal, active interest in what it is saying. Our own values, background, knowledge, and ideas can influence what we perceive, and our attitudes can make a great deal of difference to the way that we use language. If we already have an interest in something, we are more likely to notice information which links to it: our own individual experiences create mental sets, which mean that we are far more ready to process some kinds of information than others.

Social factors in cognition

It isn't possible, either, to ignore the role of social factors* in cognition. We are all members of a society, and unconsciously we absorb the assumptions of that society as we grow up. Research into language has shown us how people who grow up in different cultures often have very different ways of expressing themselves. The language that we use, with the 'world-map' that it contains, colours how we see and understand things, even if it doesn't actually determine it. People are also affected by the smaller social groups that they belong to, and the shared values and ideas which these involve can have an effect on cognition.

Cognition as a basis for understanding the world

Together, these five cognitive processes of perception, attention, thinking, memory and language form the basis for how we understand the world. They also underlie more sophisticated cognitive functioning like reading, or social understanding and shared beliefs. However, as we have seen, these processes don't take place just as automatic, information-processing routines: they work with many other aspects of human psychology, contributing their share towards making us who we are.

1. Describe two ways that physiological factors can affect cognition.
2. How may our expectations affect what we perceive?
3. In what way may social factors influence cognitive processes?

FURTHER READING

BADDELEY, A. (1983) *Your Memory: A user's guide*. Harmondsworth: Penguin. [A 'coffee-table' Penguin, well-illustrated and accessible, which looks at different aspects of memory. Somewhat 'bitty' in its approach, but useful for dipping into.]

CLAXTON, G. (1988) *Growth Points in Cognition*. London: Routledge. [A set of chapters written by major figures in the field, and summarizing whole areas of current research in cognitive psychology. Very useful.]

ELLIS, A. and BEATTIE, G. (1985) *The Psychology of Language and Communication*. Hove: Erlbaum. [A readable and thorough survey of issues in language research.]

EYSENCK, M.W. and KEENE, M. (1990) *A Student's Handbook of Cognitive Psychology*. Hove: Erlbaum. [A useful and comprehensive survey of the current state of cognitive psychology, including much recent research, but not much about the historical development of the topic.]

GREENE, J. and HICKS, C. (1984) *Basic Cognitive Processes*. Milton Keynes: Open University Press. [Like many Open University texts, this is replete with exercises and tasks for working on your own, and provides a good route for further self-study in this area.]

GREGORY, R.L. (1979) *Eye and Brain*, 3rd ed. New York: McGraw Hill. [An ever-popular, well-illustrated book outlining some of the major areas in the psychology of visual perception up to about the late 1960s. Doesn't include much recent research, but can provide a good grounding in this topic.]

HAYES, N.J. and ORRELL, S. (1987) *Psychology: An Introduction*. Harlow: Longman. [Contains several chapters which will outline basic theory and evidence in cognitive fields, although not up-to-the-minute research.]

JOHNSON-LAIRD, P.N. (1988) *The Computer and the Mind: An introduction to cognitive science*. London: Fontana. [A lucid introduction to basic approaches and research in cognitive science.]

KENNEDY, A. (1984) *The Psychology of Reading*. London: Methuen. [A very readable 'tour' of the different aspects of how we go about reading, including the question of skilled reading and reading problems, as well as the process of learning to read in the first place.]

LYONS, J. (1981) *Language and Linguistics: An introduction*. Cambridge: Cambridge University Press. [A useful and clear reference text summarizing the major areas of work within the discipline of linguistics.]

MATLIN, M. (1983) *Cognition*. New York: Holt, Rinehart & Winston. [A textbook which explains basic cognitive processes clearly and thoroughly. Highly recommended, but not always easy to find.]

NEISSER, U. (1976) *Cognition and Reality*. San Francisco: W.H. Freeman. [A readable discussion of the perceptual cycle, and how we select what we will pay attention to from our perceptual environment.]

NEISSER, U. (1982) *Memory Observed*. San Francisco: Freeman. [An edited set of readings looking at how 'real-life' memory works, including several 'classic' discussions.]

SMITH, P. (1985) *Languages, the Sexes, and Society*. Oxford: Basil Blackwell. [A survey of how sexist language and other aspects of our use of language in society affects both our cognitions and our social behaviour.]

STRATTON, P. and HAYES, N.J. (1988) *A Students Dictionary of Psychology* London: Edward Arnold. [Explicitly written for A Level Psychology Students, this contains full explanations of cognitive terms and ideas.]

TAYLOR, I. and HAYES, N.J. (1990) *Investigating Psychology*. London: Longman. [A resource book containing 100 short readings, exercise questions and other material useful for the student studying at home, or for classwork. Includes chapters on cognition, research skills, and effective study skills.]

THOULESS, R.H. (1974) *Straight and Crooked Thinking*, 3rd ed. London: Pan. [An invaluable guide to logical errors and pitfalls in argument, based on the psychology of thinking. Not only useful as background reading for understanding thinking and problem solving, but will also help you to learn to argue clearly in your own essays.]

Some other texts are recommended in the Tutor's Notes accompanying this Unit.

REFERENCES

Students studying psychology at pre-degree level, whether in schools, FE colleges or evening institutes, seldom have access to a well-stocked academic library; nor is it expected that they will have consulted all the original references. For most purposes, the books recommended in Further Reading will be adequate. This list is included for the use of those planning a full-scale project on this topic, and also for the sake of completeness.

There are relatively few references in this text, as the idea is to give a general overview which will be followed up in detail in the other Units of the series. However, those which are mentioned can be located as follows:

BERLIN, B. and KAY, P. (1969) *Basic Colour Terms: Their universality and evolution* Berkeley & Los Angeles: University of California Press.

BERNSTEIN, B. (1973) Social Class, Language and Socialisation. In: V. Lee (Ed.) (1979) *Language Development*. London: Croom Helm/Open University.

CRAIK, I.F.M. and LOCKHART, R.S. (1972) Levels of processing: a framework for memory research *Journal of Verbal Learning & Verbal Behaviour*, (11), 671-684.

GIBSON, J.J. (1979) *The Ecological Approach to Visual Perception* Boston: Houghton Mifflin.

GREGORY, R.L. (1963) Distortion of visual space as inappropriate constancy scaling *Nature* (119), 678.

HUBEL, D.H. and WIESEL, T.N. (1968) Receptive fields and functional architecture of monkey striate cortex. *Journal of Physiology*, 195, 215-43.

HUBEL, D.H. and WIESEL, T.N. (1979) Brain mechanisms of vision. *Scientific American*, 241 (3), 150-162.

NEISSER, U. (1976) *Cognition and Reality*. San Francisco: W.H. Freeman.

TRIESMAN, A. (1960) Contextual cues in selective listening. *Quarterly Journal of Experimental Psychology*, 12, 242-248.

TRIESMAN, A. (1964) Verbal cues, language and meaning in attention. *American Journal of Psychology*, 77, 206-214.

VYGOTSKY, L.S. (1962, orig. pub. 1934) *Thought and Language*. New York: Wiley.

GLOSSARY [Terms in bold type also appear as a separate entry]

Accent: a distinctive pattern of ways of pronouncing words and phrases, which is shared by members of a social or regional group.

Anticipatory schema: a set of stored knowledge and experience which is used to select relevant aspects of experience and to direct action on the basis of what is expected.

Arousal: a state of activation of the autonomic nervous system, in which the body is prepared for action by increased heart-beat, blood pressure, etc. Arousal occurs most frequently under conditions of strong emotion or energetic activity.

Artificial intelligence (AI): an area of research which aims to develop computer systems which will allow the computer to develop novel solutions to problems, or to produce other forms of 'intelligent' behaviour, such as gathering relevant information to aid expert decisions.

Attention: a focusing of perception on a limited range of stimuli so that the person is ready to respond to changes in those stimuli.

Attenuation model: a filter model of attention which proposed that non-relevant incoming information was not filtered out altogether, but rather, was allowed through to awareness in a much weaker (attenuated) form.

Behavioural correlates of attention: acts or other aspects of behaviour which accompany attention — the behaviours which people or animals show when they are attending to something.

Behaviourism: a school of psychology which was dominant in the first half of this century in Britain and America, which proposed that only the study of behaviour was objective and scientific, and that therefore psychologists should only study behaviour and should ignore 'mental' processes. Behaviourists also considered that all human behaviour ultimately consisted of links between a stimulus and a response, in much the same way as living matter consists of cells.

Capacity theory: a model of attention which is concerned with how much information we can pay attention to at any given moment. If we are highly motivated, or highly aroused, we seem to be able to take in more information.

Cocktail party phenomenon: the observation that sometimes, even when we are attending to something quite different, our attention may be attracted by a particularly meaningful stimulus, such as the mention of our own name.

Cognition: the general term given to the 'mental' processes, which include thinking, perceiving, and remembering.

Cognitive bias: a strong tendency to think, perceive or remember in a particular way, which can lead to factual errors or mis-judgement if it occurs inappropriately.

Computational theory of perception: a theory developed by Marr (1973), who proposed that we are able to recognize objects as a result of various computations, or calculations, made by the brain on the visual stimulus provided by the retina. By identifying characteristics of edges, boundaries, and figures, a series of increasingly complex representations of the object is built up.

Computer simulation: research in which computers are used to simulate how human beings behave. Those engaged in such research believe that in this way, insights into human behaviour may be obtained, although this is a contentious position.

Concept formation: the way in which an individual comes to develop mental categories, which will allow objects and events to be classified and grouped together.

Cross-modal transfer: the transferring of information which has been obtained in one sensory mode to another sensory mode. For example, using information which has been obtained through the sense of touch to make sense of what we can see.

Dialect: a distinctive pattern of speech which is shared by a group of people, often in one region. Dialects differ from accents in that they are not simply concerned with the pronunciation of words, but also include special vocabulary and grammatical forms. Linguists find it difficult to define the exact point at which an extreme dialect should be regarded as a separate language.

Direct perception: a theory put forward by Gibson, which proposed that visual perception operates as a direct consequence of the visual information available in the environment and, in real life, does not involve hypothesis-testing or significant errors.

Elaborated language codes: ways of using language which are characterized by a wide vocabulary, lengthy statements or utterances, and a lack of reliance of shared meaning. Often associated with middle-class language users.

Electro-encephalograms (EEGs): records of brain activity which are obtained by attaching electrodes to the scalp and measuring the minute electrical changes which can be detected in the brain.

Episodic memory: memory for events or happenings.

Everyday memory: memory as it happens in ordinary life, as opposed to the kind of remembering which people do for abstract laboratory tasks.

Evoked potentials: distinctive patterns of brain activity which can be measured using an EEG, and which indicate when the individual is responding to a particular stimulus.

Expert systems: computer systems which are designed to augment the work of the expert, by storing knowledge gained from many experts and providing that information in response to enquiry, in a form which can be applied to expert problems.

Figure-ground discrimination: the process of distinguishing between an object and the background within which that object is being seen.

Filter theories: theories of attention which assume that information which is received through the senses is filtered, so that the brain only needs to process a fraction of it.

Heuristics: strategies which help in problem solving, by cutting down the number of steps which need to be taken.

Hypothesis-testing theory of perception: the idea that we recognize what we see because we develop tentative explanations about what they probably are, and then look for evidence to support these explanations.

Kinaesthetic senses: internal physical senses which are concerned with the movements and states of the body. Kinaesthetic nerve fibres run from internal organs, muscles and joints to the brain, giving information about the position of the body, movements, and internal physical state.

Language: a rich system of symbolic communication used by all human beings but not by animals (in the natural state), and which differs from animal communication in a number of ways. Arguably the most important of these differences is that it does not just allow for the expression and communication of experience, but also for shared conjecture about experiences or circumstances which do not relate to the immediate physical world.

Late-selection models of attention: models of attention which imply that incoming sensory information is not filtered at all. Instead, all of the information which is received is analysed for meaning.

Lateral thinking: a system of problem solving developed by de Bono (1966), in which the aim is to jump outside the immediately apparent boundaries of the problem, and to solve problems by tackling and challenging unspoken assumptions.

29

Levels of processing theory: a model of memory which suggests that memory can be stored at different 'levels', depending on the extent to which it has been processed cognitively when the memory was first laid down. This theory proposes that the reason why some memories are quickly forgotten is because they were not processed very much in the first place; not because they went into a different 'short-term' memory store.

Linguistic relativity hypothesis: in its 'strong' form, this is the idea that thinking is entirely dependent on language, so that a society which does not have a word for a particular concept will not be able to entertain that concept. In its 'weak' form, this idea holds that the words available within a given culture or social group will shape that group's thinking, such that if there is no word for a concept, it will be harder for members of that group to conceptualize the idea.

Linguistic universals: the observations that there seem to be some descriptions which are common to all languages, and which may represent fundamental features of human experience. There are not very many of these, and they tend to relate to experiences which have a direct link to physiological processes, like the experience of perceiving colour.

Logic: a symbolic system of deduction which operates strictly according to established rules. It is a common assumption that logic is the only 'correct' way of thinking, but studies of human problem solving show that effective means of solving problems which are to do with human beings may involve stepping aside from strict logic and including wider forms of knowledge, like awareness of social conventions.

Memory: the whole process of encoding information in such a way that it can be represented mentally, stored for a period of time, and then retrieved on a subsequent occasion.

Mental set: a state of mental 'readiness' to receive certain types of information or to think in a certain kind of way.

Motivational factors: factors which are concerned with what drives people's behaviour, or motivates them to act in a certain way. Motivations may vary from physiological ones, like hunger or thirst, to social or idealistic ones, like the quest for recognition.

Parallel distributed processing (PDP): systems of computer simulation which have attempted to imitate human thinking by operating several different sequences of actions at the same time, all interlinking with one another. Sometimes known as 'connectionism'.

Perception: the process of interpreting and making sense out of information which is received through the senses.

Perceptual constancy: the mechanisms which we use to make sense of the changes in the visible image which we receive when the same objects are seen from different angles, different distances, or under different lighting conditions. The brain automatically compensates for the changed visual image, such that the object itself is perceived as being constant or unchanged.

Perceptual cycle: a cycle outlined by Neisser, which described how people actively select information from their environment on the basis of anticipatory schemata which they have formed from prior information, and from their wider knowledge of the world. The information which is selected in turn comes to modify and to direct the *schema*, so completing the cycle.

Physical characteristics: the physical characteristics of a stimulus relate to such factors as the direction it is coming from, the nature of the stimulus itself (what it sounds like, etc.), or how frequently it takes place. This contrasts with its psychological characteristics, which might include, for example, its meaning, or how familiar it is.

Physiological correlates of attention: physical changes which occur when someone is concentrating on, or paying attention to, something. Among other effects, these include changes in heart rate and blood pressure.

Representation: the process of storing information mentally, which may involve changing its form into images or symbols, or incorporating it into existing knowledge structures such as schemata or scripts.

Restricted codes: ways of using language which are characterized by a relatively limited vocabulary, increased use of tone of voice as an indicator of meaning, and an assumption of shared knowledge between the speaker and the listener. Restricted codes have been shown to be associated more with working-class subcultures, and it is important that the use of restricted codes of language should not be taken to indicate lower cognitive ability.

Schema: a hypothetical cognitive structure which is thought to incorporate knowledge and plans for action, such that they can be used to direct activity and behaviour. (The plural of schema may be either 'schemas', or 'schemata', depending on the writer or the context).

Scripts: Well-established plans and outlines used to direct behaviour and to predict what the behaviour of others will be in specific familiar circumstances. Scripts are often thought of as being a special type of *schema*.

Semantic memory: memory for 'how to do things' — like how to use language, how to ride a bicycle, or how to read. This is a type of memory which appears to be fairly robust, often surviving serious head injury, unlike *episodic memory*.

Sensory mode: a channel through which sensory information is received. In terms of the receiving of external information, there are five major sensory modes, corresponding to the five senses of vision, touch, taste, smell, and hearing; but there are also *kinaesthetic sensory modes* which are concerned with internal information from within the body.

Signal factors: factors which are concerned with the characteristics of the signal itself, like how bright it is, or how often it occurs.

Social factors: factors which are concerned with interactions with other people, either singly or in groups. Social factors may include social conventions or learned social habits, and so may influence behaviour even when there are no other people immediately present.

Sustained attention: the study of how long an individual can concentrate on a single stimulus or display before they begin to make errors. This is also known as the study of 'vigilance'.

Thinking: the mental processes involved in reasoning, problem solving, and the attempt to make sense out of circumstances or events which happen to us, or which we hear about from others.

Two-process theory of memory: an approach to memory which suggests that there are two distinct types of memory store: one which holds information for only a very brief period of time, and the other which stores information for longer periods. This should be contrasted with the *levels of processing* approach.

Verbal deprivation: the theory that certain social groups would be educationally or cognitively disadvantaged because they used restricted codes of language. This theory depended on the linguistic relativity hypothesis, seeing thinking as entirely dependent on language, and the linguistic deprivation model was challenged accordingly.

Vigilance: see *sustained attention*.

Working memory: a model of memory which assumes that, when we are using memory to think about something, we operate rather like a computer and 'load' the information into a special working memory store, so that we can then use it and work with it.